Our World
of
Words

Poems by
Chandler's Ford Children

Edited by Moira Clark

THE MERDON MARQUE

Published by
The Merdon Marque
11 Swanton Gardens,
Chandler's Ford,
Hampshire
SO53 1TP

First Published in Great Britain by
The Merdon Marque 1997

Printed and bound by

The Romsey Print & Design Company
Mayflower Close,
Chandler's Ford Ind. Est.,
Chandler's Ford,
Hampshire
SO53 4AR

ISBN 1-872340-04-0

Contents...

Introduction

This year has been a very special year for poetry.

National Poetry Day on Thursday October 9th saw a display of over 600 poems by Chandler's Ford schoolchildren in the Methodist Church's 'Chalk Room'. The event was funded by the New Forest Poetry Society's 'Youth Development Scheme', made possible by a lottery grant.
There were more than 300 interested and delighted visitors during the day who wrote their individual remarks in a comments book. It was such a success that I decided, instead of losing all the poems back to their respective schools, to put a collection together into a book.
This collection features some of the poems by children from nine local schools and shows the wealth of talent that we have in our young people. There are poems of outrage at the condition of our world, the joys and the heartbreaks in the animal world, poems about relationships, the bright and colourful poems of our natural environment and the thought-provoking poems about books and the magic of words. What you will find in these pages is truth and sincerity, concerns and pleas, but above all you will find 'word magic' from our children.
I hope you will find something which will move you, make you laugh or make you think. Whatever you find in these young poets' work - enjoy it!

Moira Clark

'Friends'

from

Fryern

Junior School

Friends

Something
to
enjoy
like
my
friend
Jacob.

He's
my
friend
to
the
end.

Peter Marriner (8)

I Love My Teddy

He is my best friend.
I take him to bed with me
and he can hug me in bed.
He can sit up with me
and he can sleep with me
but he can't talk to me,
he can't play with me,
he can't ride with me,
but he's with me all the time
and he can watch things with me
because he is my best friend.

Bobby Neill (8)

Pet Hamster

I love my little hamster,
He is fat
And full of fluff.
He sleeps all day and plays all night
Oh, I wish I could be like that.

I clean his cage
And change his bed.
He makes me laugh
For he chews his bed and spits it back out.
Oh, I don't want to be like that.

I love my little hamster
But I think I would rather be me.

Charmaine le Saux (8)

My Best Friend Anna

My Best Friend
is Anna.
I like the way
she walks.
Anna always
uses her manners.
I will always like her.

Naomi Fitchett (8)

Real Friend

My best friend is Sarah; she is really kind to me
soon we'll have more friendship you'll see.
Tonight I'm going to her house for tea,
like I said, she is so kind to me.

Sarah has dark hair, nearly like mine
Sarah has lovely hair, it always shines.

Next year at school we will be in year 5
I hope she will still be my friend.
I do think she will still be my friend
because then she would be a real friend.

Nicola Shields (8)

My Friend Is A Dinosaur

I went to school one day
it was show and tell.
Mr Taylor said, "Where's yours, Sean?"
"I left it outside," I said.
"Why?"
"Because it wouldn't fit through the door.

It's a dinosaur."
That's my friend.

Sean Coleman (8)

4

My Acrostic Poem

Friends are wonderful and they're joyful.
Rain makes you sad but friends make you happy.
In the playground you're sad, a friend comes up to you;
makes you happy.
Elephants make you joyful but I am already joyful.
Nicholas pulls my hair but I don't care.
Dogs make you happy and lick your face.
Sun makes you happy but rain makes you sad.

Joanne Matthews (9)

Be My Friend

I need a friend,
Please be my friend.
I need a friend;
Please be my friend.

Talk to me at least.
All I do is walk on my own.
I'm always bored at playtime.
I need a friend;
Please be my friend.

I need a friend beside me
To help me on my work.
I need a friend to talk to;
Will you be my friend?

Emma Dowell (10)

My Best Friend

I have a friend called Kelly;
she is like a sweet juicy apple.
Sometimes we stay together,
sometimes we break up
but then we get back together again.
I have lots of friends;
Chantal
Leah
Sasha.
I always play with them
unless I break up with them but I still get back together.
Chantal is like a banana;
she is tall and thin.
Leah is like an orange;
she is round and juicy.
Sasha is like a red rosy apple
because she has a smile every morning and afternoon.
Everyone has a friend.

Rebecca Blake (9)

Friends To The End

We will be friends
To the very end
Please be my friend
Don't drive me round the bend.

I need someone to comfort me
Someone to be there
A 'she' or a 'he'
Please be my friend.

I'm all alone
So please be here
Even on the 'phone
Please be my friend.

I've got no friends
Not even one
I need a friend
I have found one!

Roopal Vadgama (9)

Hayley

Hayley is my best friend
I hope our friendship will never end
Together we always play and have good fun
Whenever I need her, Hayley will come.
She makes me laugh and feel very glad
She is the best friend I have ever had.

Rachel Anstee (8)

It

Everything we do,
It does too.
Then everybody copies
and we get stressed too.
We don't know why
we were **It**s friend
because all **It** did
was copy us.
We will never be
Its friend again,
not even if
we need a friend.

Alexia Gillingham (10)

My Friends

I had my friends, they were kind to me,
I'd play with them, them and me
But then something happened,
I don't know what
But one day
They decided to hop.
It seemed like I was
The 'stupid' one,
I walked away from everyone.
You may say, "Don't worry,
You've got a girlfriend,"
But that's something else;
All the time together we spend.
I'm getting back together we a so-called friend,
I hope we'll **all** be friends in the end.

Philip Horton (10)

Lost Friend

I remember when I lost my friend
It drove me round the bend
But I turned the corner
And there she was
So I did not really lose her at all.

Emma Dingley (10)

Friends

I have a best friend called Laura,
I think she's really cool,
We work with each other in class
and meet up after school.
The other day
at the beginning of play
as we walked around and talked,
I suddenly thought
how great it is
to have a best friend like Laura.

She's quiet and clever,
generous and shy,
sometimes we are total opposites
and then I wonder why;
why Laura Colville is one of my bestest friends,
along with Katy and Jo,
it's strange
but I think
it's just the way life has to go.

Stacey Grist (11)

I Like You

When you are there,
I am there.
I look up to you
like an eagle in the sky.

I am your servant and
I am your slave.

I will always be there for you,
If you are there for me.
If you're feeling down,
I will cheer you up.

I like you.
Will you be my friend?

Gemma Pinkney (10)

Friends

There was a young man called Joe,
Who was very friendly with Po.
She was a Teletubby
And also very chubby
And she finally had to go.
That was the friend of Joe.

Philip Carpenter (8)

Need A Friend

Need a friend.
Will you be my friend?
To play and comfort me.
I need someone to be kind and caring;
Listen to me when I'm talking.
When I'm lonely I feel really sad.
Everyone in class has a friend;
I don't have one.
When I go home
Everyone has a friend to walk with;
I don't have one.
They are always picking on me,
Calling me names.
I don't take any notice of them;
I just walk on.
I talk to myself as I walk down the streets.

Claire Waters (9)

My Friend

My friend James is so tall
He is like a brick wall.
At football
He makes the ball fly
Like a cannonball;
There is not much difference at all.

Luke Shaw (10)

Lauren And Laura

I have a friend called Lauren;
She goes to footy with me.
We play and play
till the end of day
and by that time it's dark.

We saw some bats,
we saw some rats
and she jumped up a tree.
She said she hates them both,
unlike me.

She's coming to my party,
that's at the end of the year,
I've decided Laura can come -
if she wants to, that is.

Laura's quiet,
Lauren's noisy,
Laura's shy,
Lauren's not -
but then who is, at a party?

Joanne Hindle (10)

I Haven't Seen You For Ages

I haven't seen you for ages
And I remember that day
When I got into our car
And I went away.

I hope you're really happy.
If you're wondering;
I am too.
I hope you really miss me
Because I really miss you.

I hope the day comes sooner,
When I'll see you again.
I hope the day will come sooner,
When I'll see your face again, Ben.

Your face will have changed,
I know that.
Mine will have changed,
of course.
I hope I will see you sooner
And end that uncontrollable force.

You had a very big house,
When I saw you last,
You also had very strong legs
That could run so very fast.

You could beat me at football,
Thrash me at running too,
I remember that day
When our friendship was very new.

We vowed to keep a promise,
when one of us had gone
But none of us kept that promise
So our friendship is so nearly torn.

Andrew Reade (10)

Friends

I have some friends who play with me,
I have some friends who care for me,
If I'm in trouble, I need only shout
And those friends I have will help me out.

The friends I have are kind and good,
They treat me like all friends should,
When I am down and feeling sad,
They say, "Cheer up, it's not that bad."

some friends are girls and some are boys
And when we play we make a noise,
If you've no friends with whom to play,
Go and make some straight away.

Graham Wilkins (10)

Good Old Dad

I went to call for Ben, so we could build a den.
First we climbed a tree, then his mum called him for tea.
I said, " See you after, then," so I went to call for Dan
but he said, " I'm off to see my Gran."
I went to call for Ash but he was in a rash.
I went to call for Rick and he showed me a new trick
but he couldn't come out because he was going fishing for trout.
Help! Who do I play with?
I returned home to Dad, he saw that I was sad.
He said, "Get your bat from the hall. Let's go play ball."
Good old Dad! I was no longer sad but glad.

Matthew Curson (10)

16

'Colours'

from

Hiltingbury

Junior School

Autumn Time

Autumn leaves begin to fall;
brown, red and orange.
Pink sky in the morning,
everyone is happy.
The frost sparkles on the trees,
silver fireworks go bang at night
when people are asleep.
It begins to get dark earlier,
so snuggle up in your bed,
ready for another Autumn ahead.
The golden sun is shining in the sky,
dark blue sky in the evening;
everyone has their lights on.
I like Autumn because
you can find conkers on the path.
I like the colour brown because conkers are brown.

Maddie Ashton (7)

Leaves Are Falling

I go crunching through the brown, crispy leaves.
All the yellow leaves are floating down
and turning very brown.
My red bush leaves are falling off my tree.
A lot of green chestnuts are falling off the trees.
I put my green coat on in the Autumn.
When it is sunny, I take my green coat off.
When it goes cold, I put my yellow woolly hat on.

Katherine Whittington (7)

18

Red Is...

Seeing a lovely sunset,
The bright, red fire,
The red blood dripping out of my grazed knee,
Posting a letter in a red post box,
Red poppies growing in a field,
Roses, roses, lovely, red, red roses.

Harriet Pyatt (8)

Autumn

At the end of Summer,
Autumn leaves are brown.
When the leaves fall off the trees
and go purple and mouldy.
Fireworks, fireworks burning bright,
see the gold and silver light
shine, shine bright.
I love to kick leaves;
orange, yellow, green,
leaves gold and golden.

Daisy Waite (7)

Red Is...

Saints, Liverpool and Man. United home kit,
Red stamps in the post box,
An army of red ants passing by,
Shining rubies in the Queens' crown,
Poppies to remember people dying in the war.

Andrew Kearney (7)

Autumn Is Everywhere

It's crispy, it's brown,
it's red, it's orange,
it beautifully falls to the ground
so very gracefully it lands.

There's a whole tree
of them to fall to the ground;
they're leaves of a chestnut tree
that are going brown.

Gold, silver fireworks
fly through the sky,
shining bright,
burning the Guy.

Beautiful flames burning black, smoky.
Dark, dark nights full of bright light.

Georgina Lawrence (7)

20

Fireworks

The golden fireworks whizz
around in the sky.
Browny-golden, crispy leaves
fall on the ground.
I love firework night with its
golden, Catherine wheels
making the sky all pretty.
The Guy goes up in flames
which are goldeny-orange-yellow colour.
The trees are bare and yellow now
and everyone is in bed under the black sky.

Natalie Davey (7)

Autumn

In the forest I go,
leaves are going brown.
When we go to bed
the trees say to the leaves,
"Blow off. I am having new leaves,
the old leaves are brown and gold."
Children having parties in the warm,
outside the leaves are going brown
and orange and red and golden.
The fireworks; rockets go like this:

BANG! WHOOSH!
When you tread on the leaves
they go crackle, pop.

Keri Darrock (7)

Red Is...

Poppies swaying from side to side,
Traffic lights telling us to stop,
Strawberries ready to pick,
A fire engine going out to work,
Home-made jam ready to eat,
Lipstick sitting on the shelf with nail varnish beside it,
The blood from my tooth,
The paint in the art shop.

Hannah Milles (8)

Autumn

The bonfire is crackling still
and the Autumn leaves are changing
from green to the lovely yellow and red.
The bonfire is still crackling
but now it's time for the fireworks
LOOK!
There goes the first one; it's orange.
The bonfire is crackling still
and the first firework was a Catherine Wheel.
The bonfire is crackling still,
the Autumn is goldish,
leaves have all changed from green
to red and orange - Lovely!

Chelsey Harvey (7)

22

Red Is...

A glorious sunset behind some trees,
Poppies in memory of soldiers
Little wellies for young children,
A lovely rose in my garden,
People buying red clothes,
Blood is warm inside your body,
A London bus is coming by,
I see a robin red breast.

Chloe Lloyd (7)

My Crunchy Poem

The nice green leaves turn red
and the red leaves turn brown;
all nice and crunchy.
It's nice watching the silver fireworks
and in Autumn in the morning
it turns darker
and nearly every colour
are what you get in Autumn -
Red, yellow, brown crunchy leaves.
Lovely new leaves are going to grow...

Stephanie Gordon (7)

Red Is...

A ruby hiding under the ground,
An army of red ants making a mound,
Meteors turning into fire,
Burning lava from a volcano,
Feeling bright red with embarrassment,
Ripe mangoes; very, very juicy.

Jack Barrett (7)

Fireworks

Autumn leaves are turning brown,
Black nights are turning darker,
Bright days are getting grey,
Golden stars fly through the sky,
Leaves are changing different colours
And fireworks fly through the sky.

Stephen Keen (7)

Autumn Days

Autumn leaves are gold and crisp
and fireworks are orange and red.
The leaves that I like
to crunch are really gold.
Fireworks, as yellow as a crown
and in the dark blue sky
the fireworks fly high.

Mark Singleton (7)

24

'Our World'

from

Merdon

Junior School

The Witch

The witch is black as night,
She is winter, cold and dark
In a graveyard, old and ugly.
She is a hurricane, mad and unsafe,
A witch **is** a hat,
She is a mystery show, spooky and weird,
She is onions and she will make you cry.

Kate Cunningham (10)

A Porsche

My Porsche is red.
In summertime, in Hollywood,
It is sun glasses,
It is a settee on 'Top Gear',
It is a doughnut.

Andrew Taylor (10)

The Policeman

A policeman is midnight blue,
He is the early spring time
In a police station,
He's sunny and bright,
He's a pair of big, black boots,
He is a large, brown desk,
He is 'The Bill' on TV,
He's a doughnut, fat and sweet.

Sarah Hillier (10)

My Hamster

My hamster is light green,
She is a bright, spring day,
She is an adventure playground,
She is a clear, sunny day.
My hamster is a big, furry coat,
She is a cosy armchair.
My hamster is 'Animal Hospital',
She is carrots and lettuce.

Natalie Cosgrove (10)

The Fox At Dawn

Golden light,
Golden yellow,
Soft and gentle,
Fragile and agile,
Bright and brisk,
Sunshine, shining down.

Gemma Hyde (11)

Sounds At Wembly Stadium

Sounds of footballers arguing, shouting,
Goal keepers saving,
Crowd screaming,
Sounds of the ball punting, boofing,
As I dream of Wembley Stadium.

Lee New (8)

My Dad

My dad is a brilliant red,
He is a lively spring,
He is a theme park,
He is a bright, sunny day,
He is a bright, blue T-shirt,
He is a comfy armchair,
He is a comedy act,
He is a jacket potato,
And that's
MY DAD!

Tom Evans (10)

My Brother

My brother is black.
He is late Autumn
In a witches cave,
He is a thunder storm,
He is a pair of smelly socks,
He is Guy Fawkes' chair
When the fire is lit,
He is Dracula,
He is frogs legs.

Thomas Latham (10)

28

River

The river is swirling, furling, twirling,
Hurtling down mountains,
In fountains, it sprays.

Gushing from springs,
It splashes and flings,
Eroding the banks on its way.

It always rushes, flushes, gushes,
Speeding through rapids,
Dodging through gaps, its
Never-ending journey goes.

Entrancing and dancing,
It twists and it turns,
Gradually slowing,
It bubbles and burns.

Swirling through rivers,
They started as slivers,
Is now twisting, turning -
FREE.

Nicki Shannon (10)

The Rain Forest

Rising smoke, covering the sky,
No bird could ever fly.
Orange flames in full might,
Grey smoke really gives a fright.
The rain forest will soon be a dream
Because man is so keen.
The rain forest is beautiful, of what I've seen.
Natural fires are only fair,
They set blazing fires but they don't care.
The trees falling from the endless heat
But man is just too hard to beat.

Nick Endean (11)

Poison Dart Frog

Big, bulging eyes,
Luminous skin,
Orange jelly-like webbed feet,
Blue-green legs and a spotty back,
An arrow-shaped head,
A long, thin mouth with a mischievous grin,
A slit-like nose with two holes on either side,
Sitting on a lily leaf near a pond.

Phillip Thomas (10)

The Mountain Gorilla

Black as the night,
small soulful eyes
dreamily gazing.

Enormous grey nose,
vibrant fur like a lion's mane.

Vivid jade background,
sun blazing down,
broken ancient tree in a 'v' shape.

Overhanging leaves
swing to and fro in the cool breeze.

Emerald grass surrounded by moss and nettle,
dirty fingernails full of grime.

Lauren Priest (11)

My Oak

My oak,
with its leaves that wave in the wind
towers over the house by the edge of the field.
It's like an ice-cream in autumn
and in winter it melts.

Kerri Taylor

My Grand-dad

My grand-dad is a pale yellow,
He is an early spring.
My grand-dad is a flowery garden,
He is very sunny.
My grand-dad is a pair of shoes.
My grand-dad is a soft armchair,
He is the 'News',
He is a roast dinner.

Nicola Canning (10)

City Bus

The city bus is the biggest of its kind,
Its monstrous look is never hard to find,
Its yellow eyes are very bright
Scanning the city, through the night,
Finding a passenger, it takes a bite
And spits her out into the night,
When the bus has had some fun,
He goes back home for an oily bun,
This bus never had a fight
Because he works both day and night,
This bus is not vicious -
But the taste of humans is delicious!

Simon King (10)

32

My Tree

My small tree stands at the edge of the field,
My pear tree has leaves the colour of gold,
It's like a millionaire throwing golden pennies,
Soon he will be poor.
It hears us playing.
What if it can see me?
It can dance in the breezy, autumn wind,
It sways its leaves,
It watches me and you with its golden eyes.

Greg Walker (9)

A Cat In Heaven

They take animals from us,
They certainly don't take the bus,
They stay above us for the rest of their lives,
He was our feline friend,
He never drove us round the bend,
The nasty person that did this to him,
I will always want in the bin.

Naomi Freemantle (9)

From The Source Of A River

The source of the river,
A trickling stream,
Racing, pacing and lacing,
Sprawling and falling down mountains high,
Faster and faster it goes,
Rushing, gushing, mushing, lushing,
Eroding its banks on the way,
It runs and it creeps,
It bounds and it bubbles,
It flurries and hurries and scurries,
It's clapping and slapping,
It's roaring and pouring,
It's moaning and groaning,
It glides and slides on a great, grey rock,
It bubbles and boils,
It's prancing and dancing,
It speeds and then sleeps,
It's dishing,
It's swishing and turning, twisting,
Collecting, hissing, shining and dipping,
It's spinning and gurgling,
It's gleaming and sparkling and sprinkling,
It's bending, rounding and ready to meet
Its destination - the sea.

Jenny Owen (10)

Scared Of The Dark

When the lights at night go out,
all the ghosts begin to shout,
I get squashed against the wall,
floorboards creaking in the hall.
The dark is haunting
and dark is daunting.
I don't like the dark!
When my mum has closed the door,
all the ghouls begin to roar.
I hate, just hate the dark!
When the dark and shadows come I call out,
"I WANT MY MUM!"
Then, at last, out comes the morning sun.

Louise Newton (8)

When I go Upstairs To Bed

When I go upstairs to bed,
I always seem to bump my head
and once I thought I saw the dead.
They were some ghosts eating toast
with some butter, jam and bread.
When I go upstairs to bed, I wonder what to do,
I think of nasty things and sometimes nice things too!
When I go upstairs to bed, I do what all good girls should do...
SLEEP - that's what I do when I go upstairs to bed.

Stephanie Bunce (9)

My Tree

My tall tree has a silvery shade,
lovely green leaves.

My tree is like a big waving sea in the hot sun.

It can move with the soft, blowing wind.

Harry Mielczarek (9)

My Tree

My tree is as calm as the sea.
It towers over the school
with its yellow and green leaves
high up in the sky.
Not a movement,
until the wind blows
and pushes it about.
It's like lightening going up into space,
but in winter it's bare,
alone,
until spring comes,
when it becomes alive again.

Samuel Russell-Sealey (9)

The Fox

The fox stands tall and proud,
Ears pricked up,
He is alert and ready to pounce,
His velvety, auburn coat is much needed
against the harsh winds and extreme cold,
Surrounding the fox are small shrubs of icy blue,
under a thin layer of frost.
The fox thinks,
"How can I feed my cubs?"
"When can I get my next meal?"
"Is it my turn to be hunted?"
His jet-black eyes are fixed,
like big, black buttons.

James Hopkins (11)

An Animals Worst Nightmare

You're an animals worst nightmare if...

your moisturiser's
been approved by animals galore,
you keep your six dogs
in a flat locked up on the top floor,
you keep a tiger's sleek, striped coat
wrapped round you like a shawl,
a shiny pair of croc-skin boots
to impress your mum-in-law.

Helen Smith (10)

The quincphoop

The quincphoop's round,
The quincphoop's trembly,
The quincphoop likes
To go to Wembly.

The quincphoop's wet
And getting wetter,
He doesn't deserve
A capital letter.

The quincphoop's ten,
The quincphoop's hairy,
The quincphoop can be
Very scary.

Has he got a face?
Has he got toes?
Is he human?
No-one knows.

Does he have eyes?
Does he have a nose?
I wish somebody'd ask him
'cos still nobody knows.

With the latest technology
And good 'UFO'logy,
He sure knows humans
And he knows beans,
But no-one knows
What quincphoop means!

The quincphoop's small,
The quincphoop's flat,
The quincphoop's wearing
One big hat.

He can be blue,
He can be green,
He could be pink,
Nobody's seen.

He's got a front,
He's got a back,
His current boss
Gave him the sack.

He eats vegetables
And suntan lotion,
In a very, very,
Very strange motion.

But now, of course,
Everyone knows,
Where he comes from
And where he goes...

Alexander Clark (10)

Something

Something is here
Something is there
Something is nothingness
Without a care

Something is human
Something is beast
Something is poverty
Something is feast

Something is vivid
Something is bold
Something is shelter
Something is cold

Something is this
Something is that
Something agile
Just like a cat

Something is darkness
Something is light
Something is happiness
Something plight

Something is young
Something is old
Something is everything
Something I told.

Helen Smith (10)

'People'

from

Pitmore

Special School

Tiger

Tiger, tiger walking down the street
looking for people, nice to eat,
I hope he doesn't see me,
hiding behind the mango tree.

Tiger, tiger walking down the street,
tiger, tiger looking at his feet,
the tiger cub can see me,
hiding behind the mango tree.
I hope he likes me!

Jonathan Cutts (12)

Eagles

Swooping, diving, watching all the time.

Down, down to it's prey;
that mouse didn't stand a chance
that day.
Claws were out and her eyes were blazing,
rabbits in the field grazing;
one was caught out - lazing.

Homeward bound to feed her young;
Oh it's hard being a mum!

Daniel Newton (12)

Adam Owen

Adam Owen is the best,
He helps me when I get stressed,
He keeps my feet on the ground
And then I find that I don't frown.

He is good at climbing and canoeing
And likes to know what we are doing,
We like to sleep under the stars
To see if we can see shooting stars.

His hair is blond with an under cut,
He wears top of the range, wicked stuff,
He has no difficulty attracting girls,
He's probably the best looking guy in the world.

We all live in Badger House,
With me and Adam and all the lads,
Adam plays his music night and day
To keep Rich, Linda and Mike away.

When Adam leaves, I will be sad,
Times have been good and times have been bad,
To me he is just like a brother,
When Adam goes, there will be no other.

Mike Jones (13)

My Nan

My Nan is the **best**.
She cooks me cakes
And then she rests.
She cooks me roast
And burnt up toast.

And then I sit down in a chair.
I look at the telly
And there's Tony Blair
Saying this country is not fair.

So I came back and saw my Nan
And she said, "where's your old man?"
I said, "He's still out riding."
"You're sure that he isn't hiding?"

"No, Nan, I'm not lying,
Look at that bird, floppity flying."
I went in the garden and burped
And my Nan said, "Pardon!"

Carl Sterling (14)

Antique Nan

My nan is an antique collector;
She collects pots and pans,
anything with a tiger she buys.
She's tight sometimes but not all the time.
She runs a market and makes money --
That's it, that's my nanny!

Shane Moody (12)

Bullying

Bullying, bullying
Is not fun
But there again
There is always
ONE.

Bullying, bullying
Is not fair
So all you bullies
better
BEWARE!

David McCready (13)

Stew

There was a boy called Stew
who's quite like me or you,
he gets funny looks
when he copies from books
and the teachers don't know what to do.

Back To School

In the last week of my holidays
I was feeling glum,
I can hardly wait for school to start,
neither could my mum,
Now we've been back a week
I could do with a breather,
I can hardly wait for the holidays,
neither can my teacher.

Stewart Spiers (13)

Nanny

Nanny is noisy when I'm naughty,
Adorable when I need a helping hand,
Nice when I need money for swimming,
Never turns me away when I want a cuddle -
Yes, I love my Nanny best of all.

Sean Lock (13)

46

First Day At School

Why are you lonely?
Why are you afraid?
There is nothing to be scared of,
So why are you lonely?

I'm lonely because
No-one will play with me -
ONLY ME!

Jamie Maybe (13)

My Nan

My nan is funny
And my granddad is grumpy,
We call her nan
And we call him grumpsy.

Nan gives me biscuits and milk,
Big sloppy kisses and cuddles,
She also likes to wear silk,
Her house is always in a muddle.

James Zalavolgyi-Carr (12)

My Nanny Acrostic

Natters - all day.
Alligator - she snaps at anybody who comes by.
Nice - sometimes.
Noisy - she crows all day.
Yells - she yells all day.

Terry Armstrong (13)

'Colours'

from

Sherborne House

Preparatory School

Black Cat

Black could be a forest at night,
Or a cat creeping over the rooftops,
Ink splashed over a clean piece of paper,
The face of a coal miner after a hard day's work.

Laura Ellaway (9)

Orange

Orange is the sunset glistening over the sea,
Its reflection shines over the dull hills.
A balloon floating over the clouds into heaven,
The glow of orange in a bright rainbow.
Destiny is orange.

Hannah Appleton (10)

Gold

Golden is the morning sunlight
Across the shining wheat so bright,
Earrings glitter in the night,
A treasure chest, a beautiful sight,
Rings that hold our fingers tight
And a tooth could be a golden bite.

Gina Ackroyd (9)

50

Gold

Happiness is gold, pure and young,
Sand glistening in the sun.
The reflection of sunlight on the sea,
Italy seems golden and pure to me.
Golden buckles glint like eyes,
A golden eagle swoops through the skies.
Show jumping colours mixed with red,
A king's crown sits upon his head.
A golden labrador running wild,
Tears from the eyes of a sad child.
Sunflowers swaying in the breeze,
An angel's halo delicate and sweet.
A corn field from far away,
Summer seems really gay.
Everything seems golden to me today.

Alice Thompson (10)

All The Leaves Are Brown

Brown are the leaves falling off the Autumn trees,
The unripe pears plummeting and sinking into soft soil,
Your hot chocolate melting away by the fire
And the trees dying in the cold Winter's night.

Carla Gottlieb (9)

Orange

Orange is the tiger's coat,
Street lights glowing in the dark,
The desert on a fine sunny day,
An orange in a fruit bowl,
A fire glistening in the lounge,
The fine sunset in the evening,
A fox stalking in the field,
A brick on the side of houses,
Amber in the traffic lights
And Autumn leaves falling.

Katy Snow (9)

White

The sparkling white snow on a winter's day,
A white misty morning, we had yesterday,
Snowmen with scarves and hats on them,
Icicles hanging from a fox's den.

Lakes that are frozen for children to skate,
White sugary biscuits that Mummy has made,
All that reminds me of Christmas, gone,
How all the eyes of children shone.

Tanya Ridout (9)

52

Scarlet

Scarlet are the lips that kiss the white cheek,
The flesh which is well whipped,
The devil dancing on your back,
A ruby on a golden chain.
Scarlet describes the nose when cold,
The cherry on a cake,
The fire engine whizzing along.
Scarlet was the apple that Snow White ate,
The strawberries on a plant,
The rainbow's best and brightest colour.
Scarlet is the startling colour that catches the eye.

Rosie Bedford (9)

Silver

Silver is a magical colour;
For glistening dewdrops,
Or water sparkling in the sun,
A silver kitten playing,
The polished blade of a shining sword
Or maybe a deep secret.

Elizabeth Jameson (10)

Brown Is Spice

Brown is cinnamon and nutmeg;
for spice and also warmth.
It seems to me like Christmas,
about to light a fire.
The scent of a pine tree forest,
Leaves around you falling.
Mud on a sea shore.
The oak, pine and beech.

Sarah Walter (10)

Red

Red is for anger as hot as can be,
A crimson tide of blood after a war,
A sunburnt face from overseas,
A poppy for Remembrance Sunday,
The devil, overseeing hell,
A precious ruby in a mine,
Lipstick on a teenager's lips,
Red hot coals in the grate,
An old Victorian brick, darkened with age,
A piranha in warm rivers,
Sunset in the Summer,
The Berol I wrote this with!

Alexandra Wealleans (10)

Turquoise

Turquoise is for flowers, exotic, gay and bright,
The Mediterranean Sea, beautiful and sparkling,
A knight's horse, decked out in fine cloth,
Or for Neptune, the king of the sea.

Emily Collier (10)

Yellow

Yellow is for cheerful, bright sunflowers,
A little, furry chick just been hatched,
Warm Ambrosia custard ready to eat,
A bunch of bananas in a bowl,
A candle burning bright,
A lemon so bright and fresh,
Vanilla ice-cream, cool and creamy,
A star-fruit deliciously tasty.

Shaira Peerbhai (10)

Orange

Orange for a fox running silently through the night,
An orange so juicy and ready to eat,
The bricks of a building towering so high
And the moon shining brightly in the night sky.

Catriona Leonard (9)

Yellow

Yellow is the colour of a banana that is ripe,
Reminds me of holidays - bright sunshine
And sand castles.
Ears of corn blowing in the field,
Fluffy chicks,
Canaries singing sweetly.
The moon -
A piece of cheese?
Zest of lemons,
Grapefruit for breakfast.
Primroses, buttercups, dandelions and daffodils.
My sister's hair!

Emily Howells (9)

'Our World'

from

St. Francis

Primary School

The Rainforest

I went to see the rainforest; it was green,
It was the most beautiful colour I had seen.
A wonderful, fantastic colour, so I say,
I am staying at the marvellous rainforest for a day.
Today the rainforest was so bright
And all because of the good sun's light.
Oh! my golly gosh, what a sight,
It is so lovely but surely it is right.
I saw a tiger, it was so tall,
Next to it I saw a gorilla that was small.
There go the monkeys, round the bend,
Oh, no sadly that's the...end.

Nicola Rees (8)

In The Rainforest

The buzzy, buzzy bee,
Buzzes around the big, big tree.
The parrot proudly squawking, squawking,
The tiger proudly walking, walking.
All the birds flying around,
All the snakes on the ground.
The rainforest is very green
And all the tigers are very mean.
All the monkeys are very funny
And all the bees are collecting honey.
All the monkeys are having a swing
And all the cubs are playing with something.

Sarah Horscroft (7)

58

Rabbit

He has long ears
and a little, fluffy tail,
he hops and leaps
across the grass.

Lucy Harris (5)

The Cat

The cat is fluffy
and cuddly
it lives outside,
it eats yummy cat food
and it runs around.

Holly Banks (5)

Fish

Shiny and gold,
eating weed,
living in water,
smoothly swimming,
swims all over the place.

Connor Stanley (5)

The Snake

The stripy snake
slithered
through the stream,
it slid under stones
to sleep.

Nicholas Harris (5)

Badger

In my garden
badger scuttles around
looking for food,
he pushes the leaves -
Crackle, Swish!

Zoe Gittens (5)

Rabbit

It is cuddly,
eating lettuce
all day long,
living in a hutch,
moving - hop, hop, hop!

Sarah Dorman (5)

The Rainforest

Hanging, stringy, tangly things;
They are creepers.
Mangle beasts are noisy, it's true;
They are screechers,
Will not stop talking.
School would not like them!
Toucan squawk, their big beaks colourful;
They fly like hens.
Minibeasts crawling on the ground,
Sloths are hanging upside down.
On tops of trees are bight, green things;
They look like crowns.
Slithering creatures slither all over;
They go **'hiss';** they are snakes.
Animals have water to drink,
Hopefully the lake is not polluted.

Matthew Boardman (7)

The Rainforest

The Rain forest is very green,
It's the greenest thing I've ever seen,
The rainforest is very tall.
Like a giant, leafy school,
Just watch the hover flies whizz and hover,
It is very wet in the rainforest,
It's not like the New Forest.

Natalie Le Marechal (7)

60

The Robin

A robin is round
and has a red breast,
she lives in the trees
near my house,
she comes in my garden
to eat her worms,
I call her Rosie Robin.

Annabelle Collins (5)

The Penguin

The penguin is black and white,
it lives in a hole, sometimes,
it needs to be cold,
otherwise it would die.
Waddle, waddle, waddle.

Abigail Evans (5)

My Cat

My cat is black and white
he sleeps in the garden,
I like to stroke
his furry back,
he says,
"Meow."

Ashley Southam (5)

Badger

A badger was digging
under the fence -
Scritch, Scratch!
He ate his dinner -
Munch, Munch.

Anwin Sheppard (5)

The Badger

The badger comes out at night,
badgers live in woods and fields,
it eats worms,
it moves by feet.

Alexander Parnell (5)

My Oak Tree

Oak tree, oak tree, you're scaring me,
I don't want to die like that man in the sky,
don't throw acorns at me today,
they drop on my head, like bombs falling down.
Oak tree, oak tree, stop scaring me.

David Jones (8)

Oak Tree

There is an old oak tree
in my back garden,
I've been watching the leaves
fall all winter,
when I sit under the oak tree
I think my mother's arms are around me.

Mark Pritchard (8)

Oak Tree

Shrivelled leaves and egg-cupped acorns
on a browny-grey branch,
stuck to a tall tree.
Hawthorn growing up its sturdy giant trunk
where big hand-shaped branches stick out.
It make me feel still and quiet,
it is full of life, like spiders making webs,
it is very alive and living.

Christopher Gittens (8)

62

You Can't Play Conkers With An Acorn

I threw a stick at a tree,
a slug fell down on the ground with a **bump -**
the slug slithered away.
I picked up the stick and tried again,
this time it went higher,
right to the top of the tree.
Acorns fell down.
I knew it was the wrong tree!

Ben Perry (8)

The Oak Tree

Acorns are buried in the middle of your frilly leaves,
the leaves are shivering on the combined branches,
the thick, white trunks are like slithering snakes,
your leaves are rustling on your long, long branches,
you are as tall as a giant's body,
you bark is as rough as crocodile's skin,
birds are nesting in your long, fingery branches,
when Autumn comes you will wilt, turn brown
and let your leaves drift.

Jenny Harris (8)

The Oak Tree

I saw a green, dark and old bumpy oak tree.
The green leaves on the oak tree
were yellow and red;
they looked scary to me.
The bark of the old oak tree
was rotten with white fungi.
I'd like to climb the crusty oak tree
but it's probably too old.

Kaitlin Boden (8)

Autumn Tree

Bumpy tree with your leaves scattering
down in their crispy, brown gown,
your rough bark, like crocodile skin,
is really a lovely thing,
your green, shiny acorns
remind me of harvest
and growing corn,
you scream when the wind blows
through your branches
but you're still full of love,
your leaves are bright green
but they'll soon turn brown
and fall all over the town,
you are a very old tree
but you're very special to me.

Hannah Lacey (8)

Walking Down the Streets Of London

Walking down the streets of London
I hear footsteps and traffic going fast,
I can hear ducks, "Quack, quack, quack!"
Someone is feeding them bread
but it sounds as though they're
making a bit of a hassle to get into their bed
and in the park nearby, I can hear children playing.
I can also hear people beeping horns in their cars
and it sounds as though they're in a hurry
to get some Mars bars.

Georgina Ife (7)

London Poem

London is busy,
London is big,
London is dirty,
London is hot,
London is huge,
London is wet,
London is dark,
London is cold.

Rebekah Discombe (7)

Pollution

The water's getting mucky, the fish are dying too,
someone dumped a tin of oil and an old shoe,
the water's green and icky, the pondweed is very sticky,
the smell of pondweed is wafting through the air,
plastic, crisp packets; pooff! the smell really whiffs,
looking down from where I am
I can see a man dumping from his van.

Tim Lomax (9)

Pollution

This pollution is getting worse,
How bad can it get?
The sea will soon come to an end,
I'm going to die, I bet.

The water's black and murky,
I get stuck in crisp packets every day
And as I'm such a small fish,
I just seem to float away.

And why I ask myself, are they destroying
this once beautiful sea location?
I have a feeling that they want it to look
more like an underwater petrol station.

All this petrol, gas and oil
Is destroying the mermaid's hair,
The sea is coming to an end,
So people please beware!

Lauren Bracken (9)

Cruel Chemicals

Chemicals are being pumped into the streams,
Happening just like a very bad dream,
Environments are being destroyed,
Motorbikes to trucks let out fumes,
It's starting to get out of control,
Can you help save our world
And environments?
Lazy people throw chemicals into the water,
Save our world from extermination.

Phillipa Gower (9)

Pollution

Pollution kills the ocean,
pollution kills the streams,
pollution kills the wildlife,
if we don't try to stop it soon,
pollution will kill the world.

but if we don't try to stop pollution,
the world won't be the place
of beauty and wonder
that God meant it to be.

Emma Brain (9)

Big Ben

Big Ben chimes,
Big Ben climbs,
Big Ben ticks,
Big Ben tocks,
Big Ben's lovely,
I like Big Ben

Stephanie Clarke (7)

London

I went to London to see
the River Thames, Thames, Thames;
It was smelly, smelly, smelly.

I went to see
Big Ben, Ben, Ben
and it was ticking, ticking, ticking.

I went to see
Harrods, Harrods, Harrods,
I went to see
Buckingham Palace, Palace, Palace.

I went to see
London Tower, Tower, Tower,
I went to see
Tower Bridge, Bridge, Bridge.

Harry Warren (7)

What's Behind My Back?

What things lie beyond?
Nebula's or aliens?
What's behind your back?

Is it blue or green?
Does it hold a stun gun?
Or...was it big and blue?

All this is answered.
Just turn around and you'll see -
Gory U.F.O.s.

Robert Price (10)

Rocket Journey

I'm in a rocket,
surging through the shiny stars,
comets whizzing past.

I've spotted Neptune;
like a dazzling, glistening star,
not that far away.

Black, empty spaces
like great, big holes to fall through
into timeless space...

Rebecca Pritchard (10)

Journey To Saturn

5... 4... 3... 2... 1...
We're whizzing off into space -
I'm feeling jumpy.

I'm floating around,
we're just coming to Saturn,
Earth is far away.

Saturn is massive,
looming up in front of us -
Now we are landing.

Jonty Warner (10)

Space Journey

Taking off quickly,
it is very exciting,
zooming into space.

Speeding past the stars,
rushing past rocky planets,
heading straight for Mars.

Coming to land now,
closer and closer to Mars -
Crash! Bang! Wallop! Ouch!

Darius Atefi (10)

Rain

A dripping tap,
A fire-fighters hose,
A blue cloud,
A rain cloud.

Wind

A windy tunnel,
A burst balloon,
Paper blowing away,
Hold on to our hoods,
Don't get blown away,
Leaves coming off the trees.

Sun

A red turntable,
A yellow football,
A pan with fire underneath,
A golden tunnel,
A round golden house,
A round hand,
A GOLDEN WORLD.

Group work by reception children (4-5)

Pollution

Pollution's coming, hurry and hide,
Over the sand and to the tide,
Lots of oil and things like that,
Lots of pollution, oh bother, oh drat!
Ugly is pollution, the sea's full of rubbish,
The sea is full of lots of dead fish,
If I could do something about all this,
Oh! I would clear up all this mess.
Nobody seems to care.

Charlotte Miller (9)

Pollution

As I swim through the sea,
I wonder how it used to be,
It used to be loads of fun
But now it's all been done.
It's disgraceful to see,
That one of the creations
That God made for me
Has been put to waste -
Will it end or has it just begun?

Bryan Coughtrie (9)

72

'Books'

by

Thornden

Secondary School

Reading

Fiction, non-fiction, I don't know what to choose,
rush, rush, I have to go, there's no time to lose.
Judy Blume, Roald Dahl, there are books everywhere,
romance, comedy, books about the fair.
The library is a quiet place,
where children read about a race
fantasy, make-believe, peaceful as can be,
imagination, enjoyment, sit back and you'll see.
Books can take you far away
where you can relax and stay all day,
your eyes get tired, you want to go to sleep,
you can't get to sleep, you have to take another peep.
Put the book down, I can't stay long
but as you leave, the adventure lasts on.

Rachel Wheal (11)

Good Book

Good book this one, can't put it down,
Lights out in ten minutes,
Must finish this chapter, can't put it down.
Mum shouts first, then it's dad,
"Put the lights out, son,"
Got to finish, I must;
Can't let it gather dust.
Good book this one, can't put it down,
One more page to go...
Good book this one,
Now I'll put it down.

Stuart Stokes (11)

74

Inside The Book

Once you open the book,
the stars of enjoyment
fall out into your mind.
They make a picture of dreams
in your mind.
When you read the words
a mystical picture
parades in front of you.
Your mind spins until
you see and hear the whole story
come to life in front of you.
The last page turns -
all the enchantment flies back
inside the book.

Gemma Burns (11)

Books

I like books with humour,
funny and weird,
I like books of horror,
An old man, a long grey beard,
I like books on animals,
All cute, furry that I can cuddle,
I like books of mystery
Which get me in a muddle,
Non-fiction books,
How framers plant a seed
So please excuse me, I want to read.

Allan Petchey (11)

Book Poem

It would be cool if you could
just step into a book,
open your eyes and have a look,
just come out whenever you like,
read about a boat or car or bike,
read about crime or horror or sci-fi
and cassettes you can borrow to play on your hi-fi.
There are lots of books to read for the lover
but never judge a book by its cover!

Daniel Heffernan (11)

Books, Books, Books.

Books, books, books,
there are a lot of books on the shelf.
Books, books, books,
Pages, pages, pages,
there are a lot of pages in a book.
Book, books, books,
Words, words, words,
there are a lot of words on a page.
Books, books, books,
Letters, letters, letters,
there are a lot of letters in a word.
BOOKS, BOOKS, BOOKS.

Robert Hooper (12)

Libraries

Libraries are full of books,
Of villains, robbers and crooks,
Of cats which creep and prowl,
Where it's so quiet you can hear a stomach growl.

You dive right into a book,
Of villains, robbers and crooks,
Your brain is doing overtime,
You can't put it down till it's tea time.

Romance, horror, science-fiction, fantasy,
Whirling on the shelves,
Librarians shuffling through the books
Like tiny little elves.

Biographies are boring to me
But someone else might like them,
I prefer romance and horror
And I like to read them in my bedroom.

Rachel Williams (11)

Being A Book

Stacked neatly on a shelf
I see the shop door open and suddenly a boy appears,
His grubby hand reaches out in my direction.
I pray silently, "Please God make sure he doesn't pick me."
He does. The boy's fingers grab my spine
And I am carried and then dumped on the counter.
A sudden thought crosses my mind:
What will happen to me?
Will I be beaten and abused
Or wrapped up in silly paper
And passed on as a present
Which no-one really wants,
Just to be ignored for the rest of my life?
I look up at the boy.
Why did you pick me so quickly?
Is it that I am on a reading list
And you have to read me
And you'll turn the pages roughly without feeling,
Curling my corners and then put me in a smelly school bag?
Or is it that you have read one of my ancestors
And know that I am the book for you?

Gregory Langrish (11)

Mightier Than The Sword

It sparkles in the eyes
And is shown in the stars at night,
The reflection of the world,
Created by what one once said,
Is mightier than the sword.
And the drops of blood that reach this place
Are of people of great depth,
That give their life, their energy, their soul
To strengthen the roots of someone else's mind,
And the drops that reach the last page
Make the two words that I dread -
These two, they spell;
The finish, the final
THE END.

Jessica East (11)

Read Yourself To Sleep

Pull back the covers
Get into bed
Blankets pulled up
Lights dim
Touch the cover of my crisp new book
Pick it up
Take a peep
Turn the page
Eyelids getting heavy

Z Z Z z z z z

Laura Hughes (11)

Books

Books are romantic
Books are adventurous
Books are horrifying
Books are mysterious.

Libraries have quiet spots
Libraries have librarians
Libraries have books
Libraries have shelves.

My favourite time to read is in bed
My favourite time to read is in the garden
My favourite time to read is when I'm alone
My favourite time to read is when it's quiet.

When I read I feel relaxed
When I read I forget my troubles
When I read I use my imagination
When I read I enjoy it.

The books I like reading are romantic
The books I like reading are mysterious
The books I like reading are make believe
The books I like reading are adventurous.

Natasha Patel (11)

The World Of Books

Sit down beside the fireside,
look into the glowing embers
and enter the world of books...

Read a tale of chills
running down your spine,
you will find yourself climbing
the steps of an ice house,
where horrors of days gone by lurk.
Open the door,
close your eyes and feel
the breeze wander in your hair.
You're standing on a coastline,
desolate and bare.
Run along the shore,
feel the sand between your toes,
wander into a cave
and stumble and fall
down and down and down until...

Open your eyes to see the golden sun
which dances on the leaves
like a carpet on the forest floor.
Wander over to a glistening pool
where dreams run free
and happiness lies in wait -
In the worlds of books.

Jennifer Upstill (11)

Eaten By A Book

Cautiously I approach.
There it is - the book;
lying seemingly innocent
on the coffee table.
I touch it.
I can feel its power
surge up my spine.
"Just a few pages," I say to myself.
I open the book.
But the moment I read the first word
I can feel it closing in around me.
I try to take my eyes off the page
but I can't.
Slowly but surely the book is eating me.
In a moment I'm inside the book,
running through the jungle; being chased.
Suddenly my foot catches on a root.
I fall.
I get up again but I'm too slow;
they'll catch me.
SLAM!
I manage to shut the book;
I'm safe.
"Never again," I say to myself.

The next day I cautiously approach the book...

Barnaby Daniel (11)

82

Good Places To Read

Good places to read can be:
In front of an open fire, warming my toes,
sitting in the sun on a sun lounger,
lying on my stomach on the beach,
on a long journey, high up in the car,
at school, in total quiet except for a cough or sigh,
on a Sunday morning at the breakfast table
with the smell of newly cut grass
coming in through the window,
late at night, snuggled under the covers
with the soft light from the bedside table -
touching the edges of the book.

Hester Cooper (11)

Imagination

A dragon up a tree
or a knight in ragged clothes,
involved in space travel;
imaginations everywhere.
Stories are wise men,
in good or bad times,
dreams alive,
either football crazy
or knowledge mad,
curious of other worlds.
Be happy,
know a lot
and read a book a day.

Daniel Rice (12)

Book

It waits on its shelf,
sad and lonely;
A solitary book in a world full of aliens.
It waits,
sad and lonely.
But look, here's a hand searching
like a spider.
He grabs it,
he reads it slowly -
entranced,
lapping up every word
with utmost enjoyment,
draining it of every last
scrap of pleasure,
loving every letter.
He places it carefully back on its shelf,
smiling happily he walks away,
leaving it leaning dependently on its bookrest,
like an old man leaning on his stick.
It waits on its shelf,
sad and lonely,
for someone else to come
and let out the magic
in the pages of the book.

Charles Gerstrom (11)

Reading In My Family

In the library it's quiet
People sit and read.

In my bedroom it's quiet
I sit and read.

In the kitchen it's quiet
my mum sits and reads.

In the bathroom it's quiet
my dad sits and read.

In the study it's quiet
my sister sits and reads.

In the garden it's quiet
my brother sits and reads.

In my house it's quiet
my family sit and read.

I read R.L. Stine
my mum reads Jane Austin
my dad reads Stephen King
my sister reads romance books
and my brother reads J.R.R. Tolkien.

Josie Talbot (12)

Can't Sleep

They say count sheep if you can't sleep
but I prefer to read a book.
Everyone is asleep in bed
and the house feels still and dead,
I lift my book quietly like a mouse
and reach for my torch gingerly without a stir,
I open my book as quietly as possible
and begin the adventure...
She's running through the trees,
she can feel it's breath on her neck;
it isn't human but it isn't beast.
I'm becoming hot and sweaty
my fingers and toes are tingling...
I'm running and running
but the chase comes to a sudden stop
as I trip over a root.
'POUNCE'
One ball of fluff
with neatly manicured claws -
it's my mischievous kitten!
Can't **you** sleep?

Louise McMenemy (12)

A Book

A book is only paper
but it can make you laugh, think and cry,
A book is only pages
but it addicts its readers,
A book is only text
but it obviously contains powers,
A book is only imagination
but it takes your breath away,
A book is only art
but it impresses me more than a painting,
A book is only a possession
but to you it's worth more than your heart,
A book never ends in your mind.

Tim Loader (12)

The Book

On the shelf,
bashed, battered but somehow enchanting,
dust-covered and faded with gold printed writing,
brush off the dust and open it up,
turn slowly browned pages, filled with curled writing.
My eyes slowly wander and so does my mind,
I turn the old pages again and again
but slowly and gently so as not to tear
the well-preserved pages, full of excitement and fear.
I wish this book would never end, so I could spend ages
lost between the pages of enchantment.

Laura Segar (12)

I Like Reading, Don't You?

I walk into the library;
it's so quiet, so silent
compared with the outside world.
It's very reserved and peaceful,
there are all sorts of people here,
from young to old, from all walks of life.

I look for a book.
What should I choose?
Fact or fiction,
horror or cartoon.
What should I choose?
I know; I'll try them all out,
see which I like and which I don't.
I'll start with the 'A's right down to the 'Z's,
I'll curl up in the corner and have a good read.
I can't put it down, it's such a good book,
it's exciting, adventurous, thrilling and fun.
More people should read
everyone should read
and take a book out,
the libraries are there
for everyone to share -
I like reading, don't you?

Simon Walters (11)

Reading

Where I read is silent
and blankets out all sound,
I don't care where I read
as long as I'm alone
and chaos is blocked out.
I read when I'm happy,
I read when I'm sad,
I read when I'm angry;
reading calms me down.
Some books seem to stare at you,
as blank as red brick walls,
some books though
spark the flame of imagination
and as you see I love these novels
and in return these novels grip me.

Hosanna Scorer (12)

The Ugly Monster

I am a monster; a big ugly monster.
I'm green, mean and love to read,
I'll read through crime books, rhyme books,
sport books, big books, short books,
long books, small books, tall books.
I need to read, I read with speed,
I'll read and read until I sleep
then I'll wake reading Quentin Blake,
I don't know why, I'm just that kind of guy.
Oh my! look at the time,
I guess I'd better say,
"GOODBYE!"

Steve Challis (12)

Prisoner Of The Book

"Come down for dinner, James."
"Okay, I'll just finish this chapter."
I read and read,
taking in the story.
Minutes pass,
I reach the end of the chapter.
"Come down for dinner, James."
"Okay, I'll just finish the chapter."
I start a new chapter
but they don't know.
Minutes and minutes pass;
I'd better go now,
but...but I better read on,
just to make sure they are okay...
"Come down for dinner, James."
"Okay, I'll just finish the chapter."
I'm gripped, I'm stuck in the book;
I've been taken prisoner.
"Come down for dinner, James!"
"I CAN'T!"

James Little (12)

Good Book

When I was in bed
I wondered and said,
"Should I go read a book?"
So I looked and I looked
and I really did look
but I couldn't find a really good book.

Then, at last, I found a good book
about a guy called Captain Hook
and a little guy called Peter Pan;
they always had fights
in Never Never Land,
so Peter could've done with a hand.

Then I looked up with a fright
to see that night was now daylight
and realised I'd read right through the night,
so I snuggled down into bed
and rested my head and fell
into dreamless sleep

D D R R I I N N G G !
Oh no! My alarm clock!

Chris O'Connor (12)

Loneliness Of A Book

Help!
I'm lonely in here,
someone pick me up
and read me.
I'm really interesting,
I'm for all ages
Quick, someone's coming!
I stick out from the rest, don't I?
She's coming over,
she picks me up,
she reads the back of me
and...
puts me back
WHY?

Michelle Ramsey (12)

Books

In a library you will find -
BOOKS, BOOKS, BOOKS.
Books can tell you how to cook,
Books can tell you where to look for
Books on flowers, plants and trees,
Books on birds and books on bees.
Different authors like Anne Fine,
Roald Dahl and R.L. Stine.
So many books all around,
So much knowledge to be found.

Sarah Gait (11)

'Animals'

from

Toynbee

Secondary School

The Big Catch

Get that line straight,
swing it behind your back,
no, don't catch it on your clothes.
Squint, flick the line out forward,
hoping for a bite.
20 minutes later along comes a little fish,
hungry for some lunch, spotted a tasty maggot.
Little fish went up and grabbed the tasty maggot,
he was just about to swallow
when he realised he was six feet in the air!

Peter Barber (12)

My Spider Poem

I am a spider,
big and hairy,
when humans try to tread on me,
I get lary.

I have eight, huge legs,
yet eight, tiny eyes,
if humans annoy me
I put my venom in their way.

I like to put my spider web
all over the human's house,
in my spider web
I get the occasional louse.

Kye Smith (12)

Bamboo Trees

There once lived an animal,
No threat to you or me,
This animal lived a simple life,
Eating the bamboo trees.

Living its life of freedom,
Not hurting anyone,
Why didn't they leave it alone just,
Eating the bamboo trees?

It knew no way of living,
It had nowhere to go,
That creature just sits amongst the leaves,
Eating the bamboo trees.

This simple harmless creature,
Waiting to be hunted,
It's happy knowing not
That one more day, one more week it has
Eating the bamboo trees.

Ryan Herbert (13)

A Tiger In The Jungle

A tiger sleeping peacefully, wakes up
And has a stretch.
Goes to hunt for food
It spots an antelope,
Lies down and charges.
The tiger drags the dead body into the jungle,
Its foot gets caught in a foot trap.
It's there all day and night,
Then it hears footsteps;
Out come some poachers.
One poacher pulls out a gun
And fires.
They drag the tiger's body
To their campsite.
The next day,
They ripped the skin off its body,
Then ripped the teeth out of its mouth,
They sold the teeth and skin to the market;
The skin as a coat,
The teeth as a necklace -
NOW, ONE LESS TIGER.

Christopher Pollard (12)

The Rhino

I am a rhino
which has hardly been seen,
I have to hide all day
cos I fear for my death.

The poachers are after me,
they want my horn
but I won't give in
without a fight.

I hide behind the bushes,
I hide behind the trees,
I hide in the mud
and sometimes hide in the water.

I have been seen a few times
but have never been caught
cos the poachers
are not fast enough.

I am a rhino
which has hardly been seen,
I have to hide all day,
cos I fear for my death.

Luke Crossland (12)

Poem

The air is sweet and fresh,
old willows drag their drooping branches
through the crystal, clear water.
In the water swim fish;
salmon, trout, graying and minnows,
all untouched by human civilisation.
The birds all sing their songs,
their songs of freedom,
their songs of love.
The hills sit there; old and wise,
watching the river and its beauty below.

Jay Baverstock (14)

Lion

Lions teeth are 10 centimetres long,
their roar at times can sound like a song,
lions can turn their fear into every man's heart,
we kill them for pieces of art,
the heart of the sun beats like a drum
as the lion eats his meat.

Lions are protected by law,
so the killings should be no more.

Nicholas Hillier (12)

Love For A Dog

At first you loved me and gave me good food,
Even when I chewed the carpet, you were never rude,
Time went by and I became old,
I was skin and bones and very bald,
You got a new pet; a ginger cat
who purred and meowed on the mat,
I tried to copy her, we got into a fight,
you locked me outside for the rest of the night,
I got cold and always shivered,
every time I saw the cat, I quivered,
I went to sleep and never woke up
and the very next day you bought a new pup.

Laura Somerville (12)

The Tiger

Fire is like the tiger
Creeping through the grass stealthily
With orange and black stripes,
Until it bursts into flames
Like a tiger's pounce,
Dangerous like tiger's claws.

The tiger waits for its prey and then spreads,
Creeping through the grass stealthily,
It hides until it bursts into flames,
Like a tiger's pounce.
When the tiger sleeps, the fire goes out,
Until the next time.

Jonathan Gray (12)

Parrot

Chirpy, perky parrot, flying round,
Chatting to anyone that he found,
Chirpy, perky parrot, rainbow-like,
Could anyone be as colourful and bright?
Chirpy, perky parrot, friendly and sweet,
Cheating and lying, you will not meet.
Chirpy, perky parrot.

Elizabeth Learman (12)

A Rat

Person:
Ah, a rat!
a filthy rat,
er look, a rat,
a filthy rat.
Get that rat away from me,
Give me a broom NOW.

Rat:
Oh, shut-up, you old hag,
you really like to nag,
so I'm telling you to shut it, bag,
I'd like some cheese please -
I would so like some cheese.

Person:
Take this, you scum -
SPLAT!

Matthew Anstee (12)

100

My Dog

My dog is black,
My dog is very fast,
My dog is very cute,
My dog is the best dog in the world,
My dog lives in my house,
My dog is the best dog in the world,
My dog lives on a farm,
My dog is the best dog in the world,
My dog lives in Hampshire,
My dog is the dog in the world,
My dog lives in England,
My dog is very black,
My dog is very fast,
My dog is very cute,
My dog is the best in the world,
She supports Nottingham Forest,
My dog is the best in the world,
She supports England,
My dog is the best in the world,
She supports Hampshire C.C.C.,
My dog is the best dog in the world,
She supports Damon Hill,
My dog is very black,
My dog is very fast,
My dog is very cute,
My dog is a black labrador,
My dog is called **GYPSY.**

Julian Neagle (14)

Frosty The Cat

We bought you today; we named you Frosty,
A nice white coat,
Lovely green eyes
And a warm little cuddle; we named you Frosty.
We gave you food,
We gave you milk,
We gave you freedom,
We gave you a bed.
We did everything we thought was right
But why did you run under that car?
You limped back home to bed,
You got better. We took you back.
We gave you food,
We gave you milk,
We gave you freedom,
We gave you a bed
But why did you run under that car again?
This time you weren't so lucky;
Up to cat's heaven you will go
With a horrible red coat.
No more green eyes,
No warm little cuddle,
No cat called Frosty.

James Marshall (13)

Sooty, My Pet

My guinea pig Sooty,
She is a very dark brown,
We got her all the way down town,
She was very shy at first,
But then we gave her a big boost,
She runs around her cage all day,
Looking nervous in every way,
She's got a sister F.M.
We've had for over a year now;
and we still think they're very cute.

Alex Venney (12)

Become

When I die, I want to be reincarnated and become a bird.
I would fly so high in the glacier, blue sky,
I would chirp and swoop and loop-the-loop.
But there is a time in everything's life,
Which makes us all dead...
But until then I'll swoop around
And poo on everyone's head!

Daniel Wareham (13)

The Animals

The big cat strolled
along the wall
with a big smile;
he knows the rules.

I am a fish down in the sea,
if you're hot, come swim with me.

I am a shark,
please swim with me,
don't be surprised
if I have **you** for tea.

I think whales are really cool.
Why kill me for my meat
when really you'll find
I'm quite neat?
Don't kill me for my blubber
or my meat.

Samantha Burt (12)

My Hamster, Nibbles

My hamster was called Nibbles,
He was the best hamster I had,
When he died last month,
It made me very sad.

He was ginger on top
And white underneath,
He never bit anyone
With his sharp, white teeth.

When I bought him, he was a 'she',
Well, that's what the shop said,
But when she grew up a bit,
I found that 'she' was a 'he' instead.

At night he ran around his cage
All happy and content,
But when the sun came into sight
In his little house he went.

I looked after him well;
Food, drink, warmth and love
But he got old and worn out
And joined the skies above.

Fiona Sheffield (12)

My Rabbit, Ben

My rabbit is called Ben.
He lives in his hutch,
He eats food all day,
He is the best rabbit in the world.

He runs around all day,
He jumps up on his back legs,
He's always eating my mum's plants,
He is the best rabbit in the world.

He is always being cuddled,
Me and my sister fight over him,
Sometimes he scratches,
But he is still the best rabbit in the world.

He will crawl all over you,
Sometimes he jumps on your shoulder,
Sometimes he bites,
But he is still the best rabbit in the world.

A lot of the time he is in the conservatory,
He always hides under chairs,
He digs his food out of his bowl,
But he is still the best rabbit in the world.

He likes to be stroked on top of his head,
He always licks my hand,
Sometimes he jumps over your feet,
But he is still the best rabbit in the world.

Louise Jones (11)

The Penguin

Down in the South Atlantic
where the seas rage high,
a funny little creature
caught my eye.

It waddles along
with a little tail behind
And two big flappers
at either side.

With a bright, yellow beak
and feet to match,
this little fellow
is quite a catch!

Helen Owens (12)

My Fish

GLUG! GLUG! GLUG!
My fish is swimming in the deep and misty tank,
He bounces off the glass
thinking there is nothing there.
Food drops in -
He goes straight up to the top and
GLUP!
All the food is gone.
Now my fish can swim happily by...

Carl Davey (12)

My Little Fluffy Bunny

My little, fluffy bunny,
Has legs that go all funny,
He wobbles to and fro,
Though he always keeps quite low.
As he eats he chews so softly,
When he drinks he does it slowly,
He plays with me so sweetly
And he always sleeps so neatly -
Or that's what he used to do.
He was walking down the street,
He had escaped from the hutch,
It must have been bad luck,
Then he ran into the road,
Along came a heavy load.
Now he's gone,
Never to be seen again.

Claire Watkins (12)

My Little Tiger

My little tiger is the funniest,
My little tiger is bouncy as a spring,
My little tiger is my best friend,
My little tiger grew too big and went to the jungle to live.
Why, my little tiger?
Why my little tiger did that evil man shoot you?
Why my little tiger?
Why my little tiger did you go to heaven?
Why my little tiger?

Daniel Safar-Manesh (11)

The Fat Little Pig

The fat, little pig rolled around in the mud
living his happy life,
the fat, little pig got up from the mud,
he had to close his eyes.

The fat, little pig didn't know what happened
but he was still alive,
instead of 5 there were only 4
pigs left in the sty.

The fat, little pig rolled around in the mud
but this was the next day,
the fat, little pig was thinking
about what happened yesterday.

The fat, little pig said in his mind,
"Why kill me for my meat?
I'll try to be kind,
I promise."

Rachel Savage (13)

The Hedgehog And The Bonfire

There once was a hedgehog
with its long thistle-like spines,
it sat in my garden
feasting on greenfly.

The month is November,
time to hibernate,
it finds a nice, cosy bush
which is really our bonfire.

Next morning I go outside,
I tear the bonfire to pieces
when I find the hedgehog,
I build a nesting site.

I've ruined the bonfire
but at least I've saved a life
of a young hedgehog
with its shiny spikes.

Matthew Deacon (12)

Look Alive, Duck And Dive

Oh please help me, I'm in trouble;
I'm stuck in this cage day and night,
when I first saw it, it was a fright.
One year I was in that cage
but one day the owner left my cage
UNLOCKED!
Now's my chance.
I flew towards the window and out;
I was free.
Free, like I'm supposed to be,
ducking and diving.
I thought I'd forgotten how to fly
but not me, not I.
Look! watch me, **duck,**
watch me, **dive,**
I'm free, I am alive.
Look! I'm alive,
I can duck and dive.
I think I'll have a sleep now,
I'll fly this land tomorrow
because...
I'm alive,
I can duck and dive.

Timothy Johnson (13)

Elephants

I'm walking through my African jungle,
knocking down trees with my tusks; so white and long.
Why, when I'm doing nothing wrong,
should you take them away from me?

Why are they used for piano keys
when they're so much more use to me?

There aren't many of us left now,
so please leave us alone.
Make your trivial trinkets
from gold, silver or precious stone.

Elizabeth Eales (12)

Demon Eyes

It was quiet, too quiet.
The deers were eating, not knowing
what was about to happen to them.
Then all of sudden a branch broke...
The deer turned...
All it could see was red, red, demon eyes.
It turned to run
but the bullet was too fast.

They are not going to use the dead body.
"It's just for fun," they say.
"There's plenty more where they came from."

Callum Ryan (12)

112

'Water'

from

Woodhill

Preparatory School

Raindrops

We are here; raindrops.
We are here to help your plants,
to give them a drink.

The River

Water comes from rain,
cold, freezing water that flows,
that grows, to the sea.

Russell Burton (9)

Weeping Willow

Weeping willow, weeping willow,
with leaves hanging down,
weeping willow, weeping willow,
you look as if you frown.

Standing by the river,
looking very sad,
staring at a rain drop
and as it lands, I hear a
PLOP!

Charles Hewitt (10)

Willow

I am the weeping willow,
I weep all the time,
I stand by the river
all the time.

Raindrops

The raindrops crash,
the raindrops splash,
the raindrops tripple
and then ripple,
the river swirls
around and around.

Jonathan Peacock (8)

Rivers

The river goes from the lake
as the earth seems to shake,
going in turns,
not shoving, not pushing,
flowing gently to the sea
where it will go and be free.

Joseph Marti (8)

Fishing

With my long rod,
I fish the river,
in the calm
I watch the reflection of me.
Silver shoal of fish,
it's better than a wish
to be all alone
just watching the water run by.
Bright green grass along the shore,
it's better than watching a bare floor
as I watch the gleaming fish
in the clear, blue water;
so lovely and transparent.
As the rod pulled,
I tugged and tugged,
then with a splash I fell -

splash, splash, splash!

As I see the fish prowl,
can someone pass me a towel?

Ranjeet Shahi (10)

Fish

I swam through tall reeds
poking out by the water's edge
when I grabbed a fish.
I was tugged out of the water
and thrown into a tank.

Peter Sandiford (10)

116

Rain

Drip, drop, splash, plop,
raindrops falling on the ground,
making puddles,
making the rainbows
in the sky.

Helen Sandiford (8)

The Weeping Willow

The tree which weeps and weeps,
it dangles with its long hairy arms.
The brown, crumbly trunk
which peels and peels.
Do you know what it is?
It's a weeping willow.

Pavandeep Birk (8)

Raining

Water is calm as it trickles
down the leaf of a tree,
swept by a gentle breeze
and it falls in the river
to create a ripple.
As the sun shines on it
the water beams.

Dariush Afshar (8)

Water World

The sun shines brightly,
the rain falls lightly,
the river swirls,
the raindrops look like pearls,
the river ripples,
the rain tripples,
there is a breeze
through the trees.

Natasha Small (7)

Raindrops

Splish, splash goes the rain
making ripples in the water -
rainbow shining through.

Blazing Sun

The sun is blazingly hot
but not all the time.
The sun is red.
The sun is danger.

Iona Clark (7)

Red

Red is bright,
red is warm,
red is blood,
red is anger,
red is danger.

Blue

Blue makes me shiver in my head
with the breeze through the door.

Matthew Ireland (9)

Colours

The blood, red sun
is blurred in the water
as silver fish make it blend in the blue.
The orange tree stretches into the sky.

Andrew Jones (10)

Blue

Blue is the colour
that makes me feel all happy.
Like the rain,
it is nice.

Sara McKay (7)

Drip, Drip, Drip...

When you're playing in the sun,
the clouds go over the shining sun
and the raindrops come.

The children go inside.
It gets heavier and heavier;
a small thunder storm.

The next day everything
is horrible and wet.

William Marks (8)

Swirler, Whirler

Swirling and whirling,
the raindrops fall,
making ripples grow,
huger and huger
but washing away
as another one comes.

Watching the cold, tender swirl
go rushing down the river,
slowly the ripples fade into the water.

The raindrops fall into the lake,
splashing and waving,
making sweet little noises;
going patter, splash, patter...

Katrin Rees (10)

120

Raindrops

Splash! go the raindrops, **splash!**
In the river ripples appear,
bigger and bigger the ripples get,
I know there are more coming, I bet!

Alexander Price (9)

Rain

The raindrops were falling down into the cold, wet water,
the day was hot,
I saw a small rainbow;
the sky was blue and it was raining.
When the raindrops fell into the river,
there was a large SPLASH!
It was midday on Sunday.
I had caught two fish.
Suddenly a fish caught hold of the rod
and started to pull me into the river
but it let go.
Raindrops were falling into the river
and making larger and larger ripples.
There was a tree in the background;
it was tall and dark brown.
The fish that I caught were the colours of the rainbow.

Gregory Small (11)

River

I am the river,
bright and clear,
gushing through towards the sea.
Fishes, toads, newts and things
dwell beneath me.

Andrew Nanapragasam (9)

Trout

It's me trout,
coming to explore the wonder
of this river;
passages everywhere.
It's a long river
and there's lots to explore;
swishing through the weeds,
exploring holes;
some don't even go anywhere.
Then suddenly a school of fish
come swimming past
making the water churn.

Daniel Sayles (10)

Raindrops

The water comes from the sky,
the raindrops splash.
When they drop,
they make circles
and they get wider and w i d e r.

Rohit Kapoor (9)

Water

A tender little raindrop
on a bright red rose,
a soft wind blowing
but where no-one knows.

A peaceful little country,
a river running by,
the rain is falling;
no-one wonders why.

Twisting and twirling,
large, blue drops from the grey sky
rush - it's raining.

Catriona Yeoh (10)

Colours

Red; a hot, shocking warmth,
bright danger and loving care.
Blue; cold, freezing, frosting blue,
blue, blue as the sky.

Jemulata Haynes (10)

The Water As It Goes...

The water and the river -
plop, plop, plop as it goes,
the water and the lake -
flop, flop, flop as it flows,
the water and the rainbow -
brighter as it glows,
the water, lake, river and rainbow
they connect -
Oh! don't those.

Zobia Arshad (10)

A Rainbow Sky

Blurry red in the sky,
getting tender all the time,
orange of a baby sunflower
blending in with the red,
sandy yellow of the sky,
never saying bye-bye,
green of the trees
and the meadows all around,
blue of the sea
and blue of the sky,
indigo colours of a bruise
never willing to go for a snooze,
violet, purple of the flower -
now it's going down under the sunset,
ready to come out another day.

Oliver Kaderbhai (9)

124

The Sun

The sun is shining brightly,
the blazing colour red
as I look through a window,
I sit up in bed.
The sunrays are beaming down,
sometimes on my face -
I love the sun.

Avneet Shahi (9)

Rain

Bumping on the mountains at sixty miles an hour,
rushing down the hill, heading for the tower,
twisting round the bends of the River Cower,
glimpses of newts and fishes of power,
coming to Victoria Falls,
angry shouts and loud calls,
the waters are scared to death,
the drops are now left.

Christopher Ward (10)

Sun

Sun is hot and yellow,
it's a bright colour.
Rain comes and the sun goes,
after that the rainbow comes
and the sun comes back.

Arun Pone (8)

Raindrops

Rain is wet,
Rain makes puddles,
Rain can hammer down,
It can pitter, patter,
Sometimes floods places
and takes a long time to dry.
When it rains, it thunders
and the rain makes a nice sound
and places get wet
and trees get wet.
The rain tripples.

Warren Cable (8)

Blue

As blue as the night,
As blue as the sea,
As blue as the water,
As blue as rain,
Not red, not green but
BLUE, BLUE, BLUE

Rikky Sharma (8)

Rain

Metal rusts with it,
the sea's made of it,
it falls in a gutter -
it's rain.

Sean Veck (8)

Red

Red as a strawberry,
Red as a raspberry,
Red as an apple,
Red a colour of a flower,
Red can be anything you want it to be.

Zara Sparkes (8)

Violet

I am the violet,
I am here,
Sometimes bright,
Sometimes clear,
Sometimes misty
when the rain comes near,
I'll never ever leave,
I'll stay here.

Bethan Knights (9)

Hot

I got so hot, like the sun
and then POP! I got even hotter.
Then I suddenly saw I was beaming
like a lazer on the ground,
I went as orange as anything,
I was beaming like fire -
I **was** the sun.

James Ward (7)

Fish

I am a fish swimming in the lake,
my home is an old tin can,
it must have been kicked in by man.
I play with my fish friends,
we love swimming around bends;
the fun never ends,
swimming round bends.
But we all know
never ever be caught by lines!

Christopher Peacock (11)

Rainbow

I am the rainbow that brightens up the sky,
I'm way up high.
I need the rain and sun to form me
but when I'm up I'm as tall as a tree.
The bright colours make me stand out.
The rain stops and then I fade.

Matthew Leech (11)

The Sun

The sun is bright yellow,
it shines right over me,
when the sun and rain mix
they make a rainbow

William Hewitt (8)

128

Index Of Poets

Ireland, Matthew 119
Jameson, Elizabeth 53
Johnson, Timothy 111
Jones, Andrew 119
Jones, David 62
Jones, Louise 106
Jones, Mike 43
Kaderbhai, Oliver 124
Kapoor, Rohit 123
Kearney, Andrew 20
Keen, Stephen 24
King, Simon 32
Knights, Bethan 127
Lacey, Hannah 64
Langrish, Gregory 78
Latham, Thomas 28
Lawrence, Georgina 20
Le Marechal, Natalie 60
le Saux, Charmaine 3
Learman, Elizabeth 100
Leech, Matthew 128
Leonard, Catriona 56
Little, James 90
Lloyd, Chloe 23
Loader, Tim 87
Lock, Sean 46
Lomax, Tim 66
Marks, William 120
Marriner, Peter 2
Marshall, James 102
Marti, Joseph 115
Matthews, Joanne 5
Maybe, Jamie 47
McCready, David 45
McKay, Sara 119
McMenemy, Louise, 86
Mielczrek, Harry 36
Miller, Charlotte 72
Milles, Hannah 22
Moody, Shane 45
Nanapragasam, Andrew 122
Neagle, Julian 101
Neill, Bobby 2
New, Lee 27
Newton, Daniel 42
Newton, Louise 35

O'Connor, Chris 91
Owen, Jenny 34
Owens, Helen 107
Parnell, Alexander 61
Patel, Natasha 80
Peacock, Christopher 128
Peacock, Jonathan 115
Peerbhai, Shaira 55
Perry, Ben 63
Petchey, Allan 75
Pinkney, Gemma 11
Pollard, Christopher 96
Pone, Arun 125
Price, Alexander 121
Price, Robert 69
Priest, Lauren 31
Pritchard, Mark 62
Pritchard, Rebecca 69
Pyatt, Harriet 19
Ramsey, Michelle 92
Reade, Andrew 14
Reception Class Children 71
Rees, Katrin 120
Rees, Nicola 58
Rice, Daniel 83
Ridout, Tanya 52
Russell-Sealey, Samuel 36
Ryan, Callum 112
Safar-Manesh, Daniel 108
Sandiford, Helen 117
Sandiford, Peter 116
Savage, Rachel 109
Sayles, Daniel 122
Scorer, Hosanna 89
Segar, Laura 87
Shahi, Avneet 125
Shahi, Ranjeet 116
Shannon, Nicki 29
Sharma, Rikky 126
Shaw, Luke 12
Sheffield, Fiona 105
Sheppard, Anwin 61
Shields, Nicola 4
Singleton, Mark 24
Small, Gregory 121
Small, Natasha 118

Smith, Helen 37/40
Smith, Kye 94
Snow, Katy 52
Somerville, Laura 99
Southam, Ashley 61
Sparkes, Zara 127
Spiers, Stewart 46
Stanley, Connor 59
Sterling, Carl 44
Stokes, Stuart 74
Talbot, Josie 85
Taylor, Andrew 26
Taylor, Kerri 31
Thomas, Phillip 30
Thompson, Alice 51
Upstill, Jennifer 81
Vadgama, Roopal 7
Veck, Sean 126
Venney, Alex 103
Waite, Daisy 19
Walker, Greg 33
Walter, Sarah 54
Walters, Simon 88
Ward, Christopher 125
Ward, James 127
Wareham, Daniel 103
Warner, Jonty 70
Warren, Harry 68
Waters, Claire 12
Watkins, Claire 108
Wealleans, Alexandra 54
Wheal, Rachel 74
Whittington, Katherine 18
Wilkins, Graham 16
Williams, Rachel 77
Yeoh, Catriona 123
Zalavolgyi-Carr, James 47